HONG KONG

WENDY BUEHR MURPHY

THE
GREAT
CITIES
LIBRARY

A BLACKBIRCH PRESS BOOK

WOODBRIDGE, CONNECTICUT

Published by Blackbirch Press, Inc.
One Bradley Road, Suite 205
Woodbridge, CT 06525

©1991 Blackbirch Press, Inc.
First Edition

Printed in Hong Kong
Bound in the United States of America

Editors: Kailyard Associates
Maps: Robert Italiano
Photo Research: Photosearch, Inc.

Library of Congress Cataloging-in-Publication Data

Murphy, Wendy B.
  Hong Kong/Wendy Buehr Murphy.
  (The Great cities library)
  Includes bibliographical references and index.
  Summary: Describes the place, history, and people of Hong Kong.
  ISBN 1-56711-021-5
  1. Hong Kong—Juvenile literature. [1. Hong Kong.] I. Title. II. Series.
DS796.H74/M87 1990
951.25—dc20   90-43869
                                                               CIP
                                                               AC

pages 4–5
Many of Hong Kong's factory workers live on houseboats in the city's crowded harbor.

CONTENTS

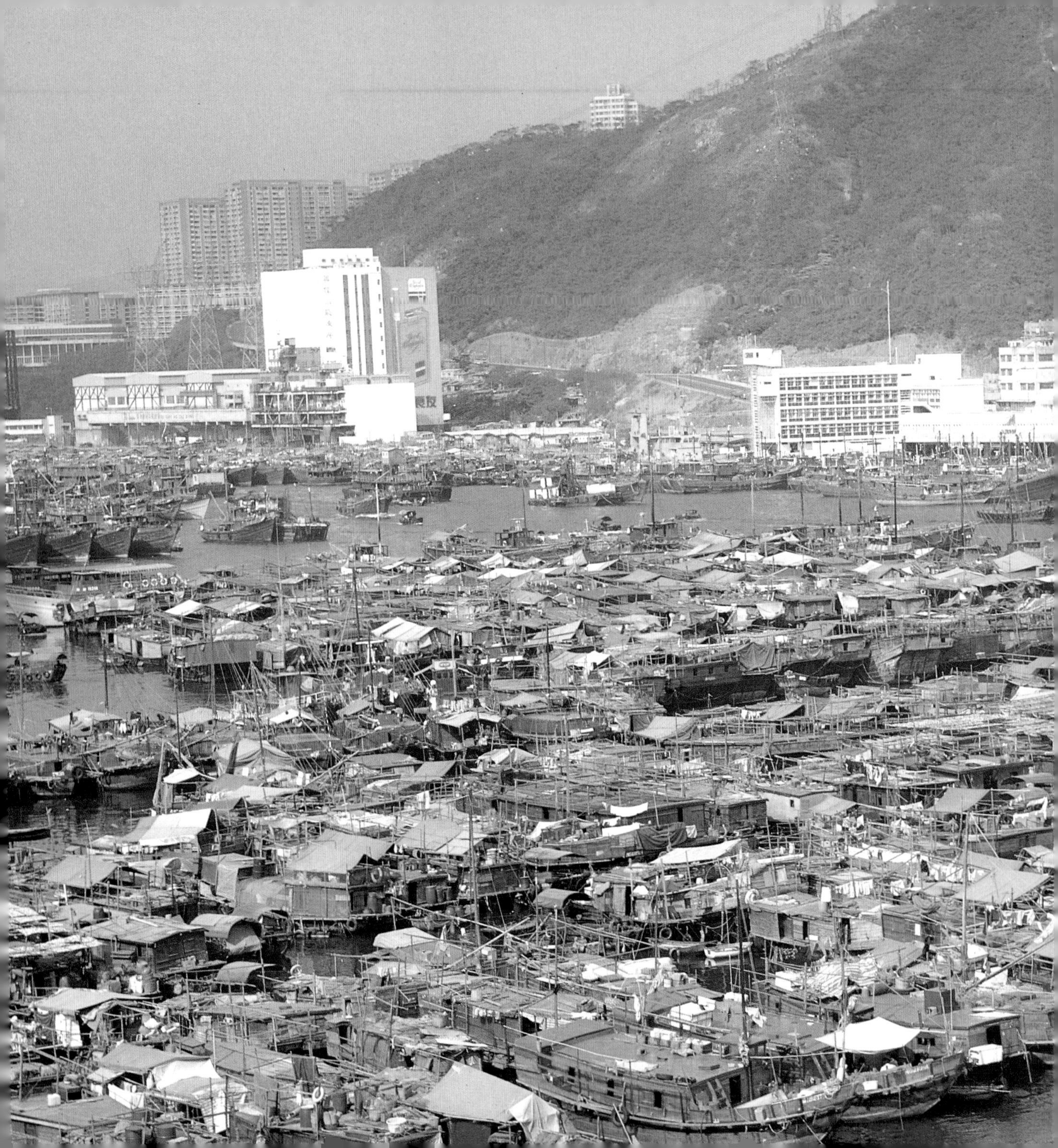

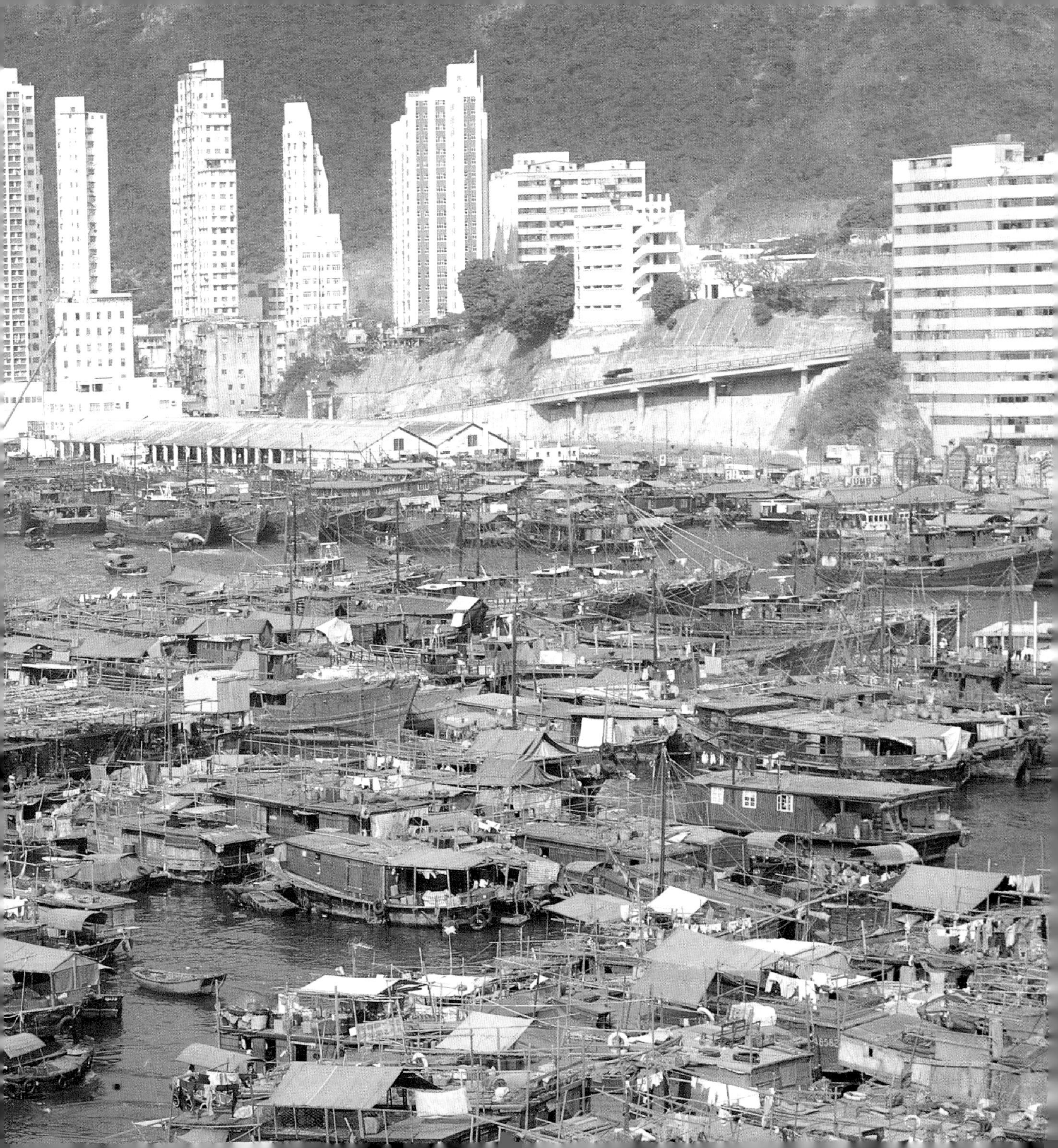
JUMBO

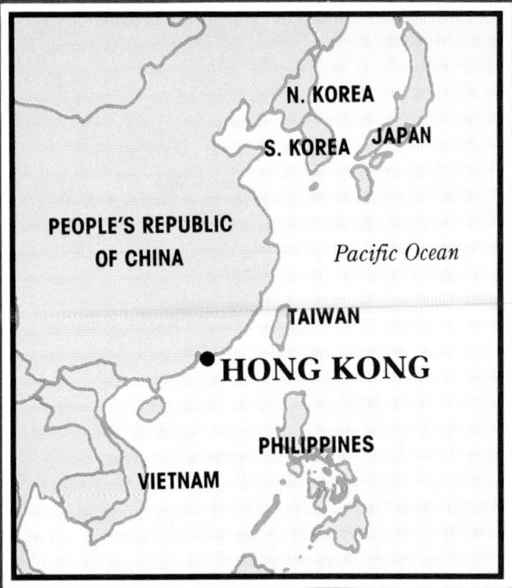
N. KOREA
S. KOREA
JAPAN
PEOPLE'S REPUBLIC OF CHINA
Pacific Ocean
TAIWAN
HONG KONG
PHILIPPINES
VIETNAM

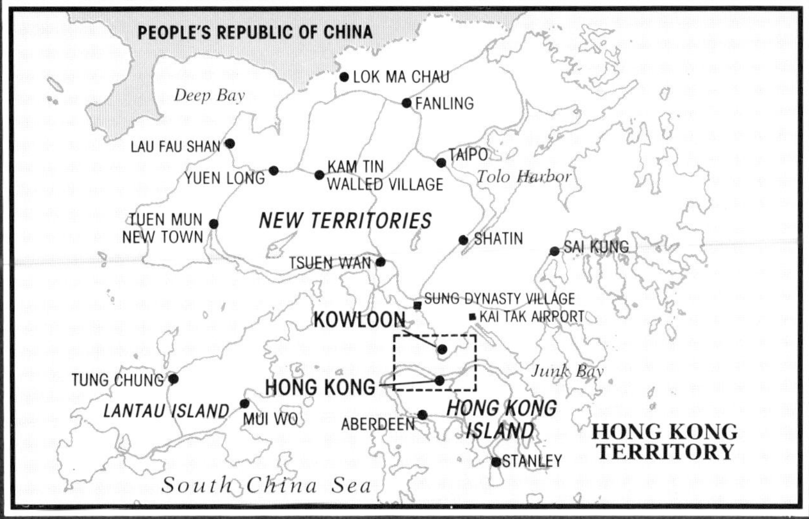
PEOPLE'S REPUBLIC OF CHINA
LOK MA CHAU
Deep Bay
FANLING
LAU FAU SHAN
TAIPO
YUEN LONG
KAM TIN WALLED VILLAGE
Tolo Harbor
TUEN MUN NEW TOWN
NEW TERRITORIES
SHATIN
SAI KUNG
TSUEN WAN
SUNG DYNASTY VILLAGE
KOWLOON
KAI TAK AIRPORT
Junk Bay
TUNG CHUNG
HONG KONG
LANTAU ISLAND
MUI WO
ABERDEEN
HONG KONG ISLAND
HONG KONG TERRITORY
STANLEY
South China Sea

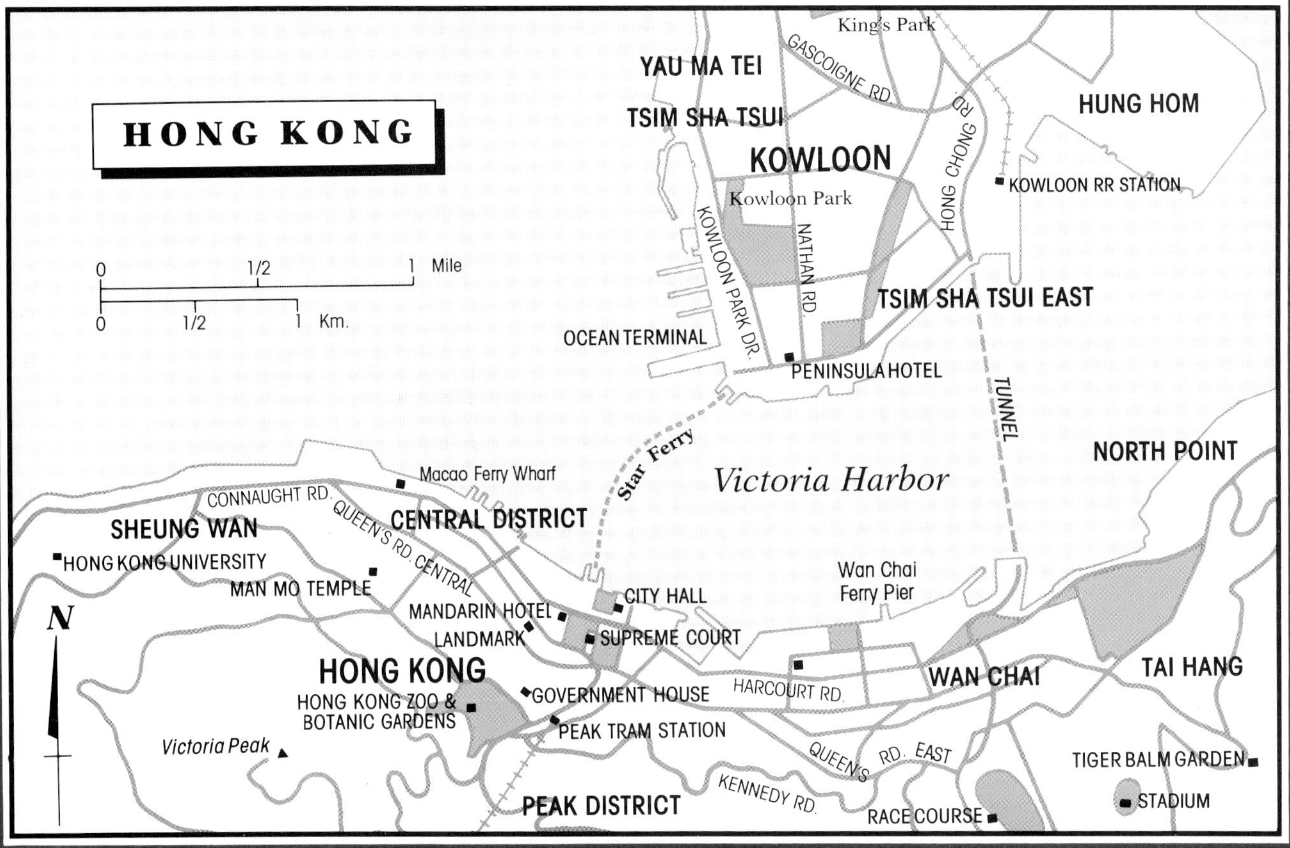
HONG KONG
King's Park
YAU MA TEI
GASCOIGNE RD.
TSIM SHA TSUI
HUNG HOM
KOWLOON
HONG CHONG RD.
KOWLOON RR STATION
Kowloon Park
KOWLOON PARK DR.
NATHAN RD.
0
1/2
1
Mile
0
1/2
1
Km.
TSIM SHA TSUI EAST
OCEAN TERMINAL
PENINSULA HOTEL
TUNNEL
Star Ferry
NORTH POINT
Victoria Harbor
Macao Ferry Wharf
CONNAUGHT RD.
QUEEN'S RD. CENTRAL
SHEUNG WAN
CENTRAL DISTRICT
HONG KONG UNIVERSITY
MAN MO TEMPLE
Wan Chai Ferry Pier
CITY HALL
MANDARIN HOTEL
N
LANDMARK
SUPREME COURT
HONG KONG
TAI HANG
WAN CHAI
HONG KONG ZOO & BOTANIC GARDENS
GOVERNMENT HOUSE
HARCOURT RD.
PEAK TRAM STATION
Victoria Peak
QUEEN'S RD. EAST
TIGER BALM GARDEN
KENNEDY RD.
STADIUM
PEAK DISTRICT
RACE COURSE

Population: 5,500,000

Size: Total land area is approximately 412.5 square miles.

Ethnic Makeup: 98 percent Chinese

Major Languages: Cantonese and English

Nickname: Fragrant Harbour

Characteristics: Hong Kong consists of 230 islands and a peninsula of the People's Republic of China in the South China Sea. It is divided into three principal parts: Hong Kong Island (about 35 square miles); Kowloon, on the Kowloon peninsula (3.5 square miles); and the New Territories plus hundreds of outer islands (about 374 square miles). Forty percent of Hong Kong's territory consists of undisturbed green, park-like land; the rest is used for buildings.

Government: Hong Kong is a British Crown colony until 1997 when it comes under the control of the People's Republic of China. The new state will have a constitution known as "The Basic Laws" and will govern itself independently for 50 years.

Main Business Activities: As a free port and trading center, the city's major economic activities are marketing and banking.

Hong Kongers have adopted many Western habits. Golf is a local passion among the affluent.

THE PLACE

"Squeezed between giant antagonists crunching huge bones of contention...Hong Kong has achieved within its own narrow territories a co-existence which is baffling, infuriating, incomprehensible and works splendidly—on borrowed time in a borrowed place."

—Han Su-yin

The five million residents of Hong Kong experience the daily hustle and bustle of city life.

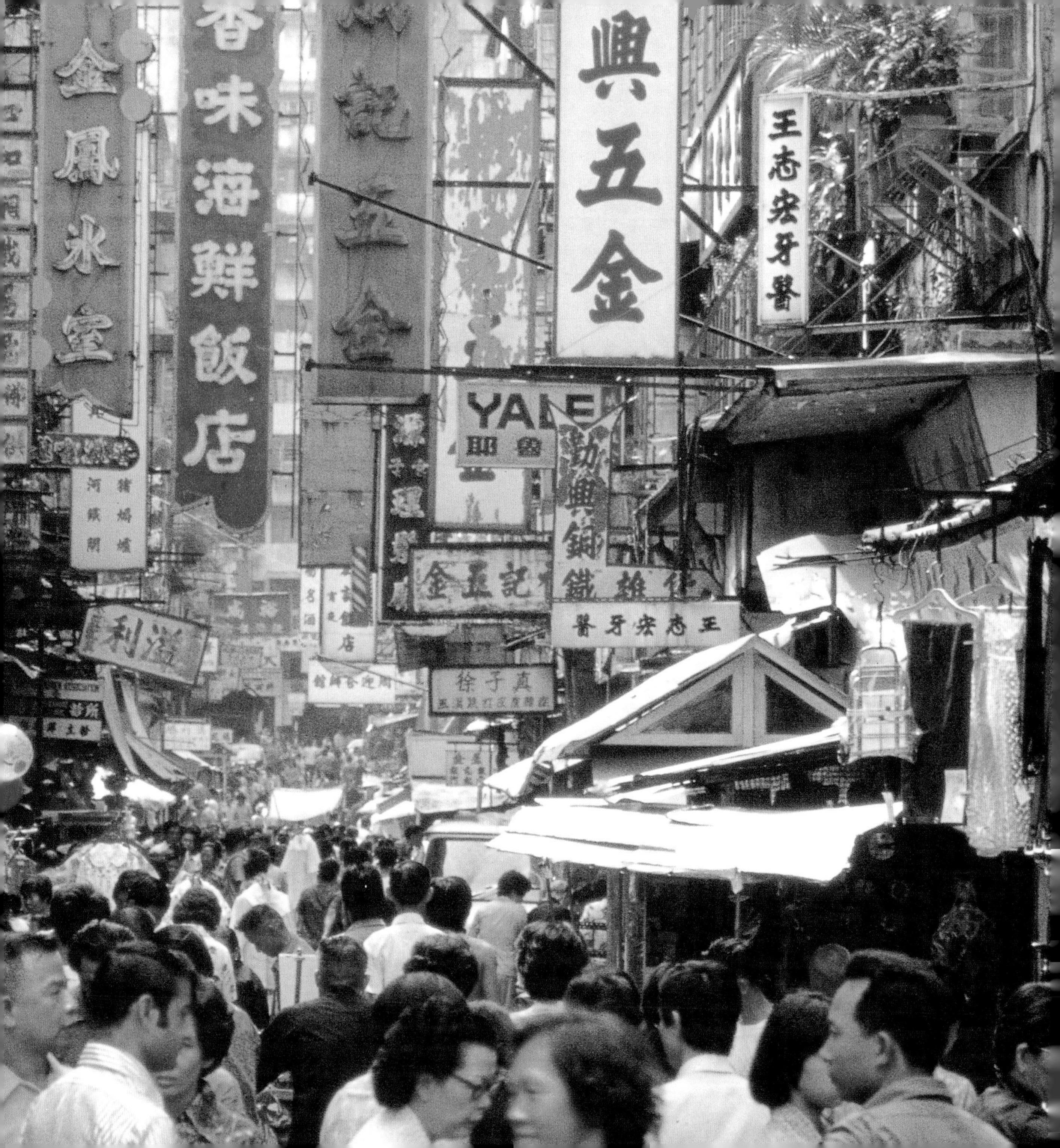
金鳳冰室
香味海鮮飯店
興五金
YALE

The British Crown Colony of Hong Kong—
or, as it was known in precolonial times,
Xianggang—lies on the shore of the South
China Sea at the foot of China's Guangdong Province. Though most people think of Hong Kong as
being a city in the conventional sense, it actually
consists of 230 islands and a peninsula, with a total
land area of 412.5 square miles. Hong Kong is located on the southeast coast of mainland China at
the mouth of the great Pearl River, which, despite
its pretty name, is quite muddy. Air travel to Hong
Kong takes about 18 hours from New York, 12
hours from America's west coast, and 13 hours
from London.

The territory of Hong Kong is made up of three
principal parts: Hong Kong Island (about 35
square miles); Kowloon, on the Kowloon peninsula
(3.5 square miles); and the New Territories, plus
hundreds of outer islands (about 374 square miles).
Of the many mountains on Kowloon peninsula,
more than twenty rise over 1,000 feet in height, two
reach above 2,700 feet, and one of these, Tai Mo
Shan, has an elevation of 3,140 feet. The mountains are known collectively to the Chinese as the
Nine Dragons. The most familiar to Hong Kongers
is Victoria Peak, which towers above the city's harbor.

The mountains contributed in a special way to the
growth of Hong Kong. Level space is at a premium

in the colony, so for many years workers have been blasting loose rock and earth in the mountains and trucking it down to the coast, where it is dumped out onto the shore and bulldozed into the ocean to enlarge the land area. This laborious process has created space for thousands of houses and businesses and additional reclaimed land is added each year. Forty percent of Hong Kong's territory consists of green, undisturbed park-like land, while 51 percent is built up with small houses and modest business structures; only 9 percent of Hong Kong is covered with the soaring skyscrapers so familiar in news photos and on TV.

Floating house in Yaumatei Harbor, Hong Kong.

The economic heart of the colony consists of twin cities that lie on either side of the harbor—Kowloon, on the peninsula, and Central, on Hong Kong Island, about a mile to the south. The two cities, connected by ferries and a vehicular tunnel, are called Hong Kong-side and Kowloon-side. The island district was originally named Victoria, after the Queen of England, but now it is known simply as Central. Here is the governmental and financial heart of Hong Kong; here also is the site of great old trading houses ruled over by chief executives still known by the honorary Chinese term, *taipan*.

Kowloon-side, across the bay, is where one can find the most and best hotels, and it has a reputation for being a shopper's paradise. Above Kowloon-side is the remainder of Kowloon penin-

sula, part of the New Territories. This area stretches northward through the mountains to the border with China.

Five hundred years ago, many of the people of what is now called Hong Kong lived aboard boats moored in the busy, crowded harbor, and thousands of them still do to this day. The vessels are called *junks,* a name taken from a Malay word meaning "seagoing ship," but few of these junks have ever

Victoria Peak towers above Hong Kong Island.

sailed in deep water. Most of them carry loads of freight and occasional passengers between various coastal points and to the offshore islands. Today they are propelled not by traditional bat-winged sails but by chugging, old diesel engines. Other junks, older and no longer seaworthy, remain instead on permanent mooring as floating houses.

The overwhelming majority of the colony's citizens live on land. With buildable land hard to find,

Food markets supply fresh fish and other specialities to Hong Kong's large population.

housing has been jammed together: about 80 percent of the people live crowded onto only 8 percent of the land area. The poor occupy tiny rooms in squalid tenement communities found throughout Hong Kong, with unhealthy conditions that make tuberculosis a major health problem. The large middle-class population lives in high-rise buildings erected on the few flat ground areas and on the steep hills above the harbor.

In front of these high-rise apartments, a dramatic lacework of skyscraper office buildings thrusts up along the crowded southern shore of Kowloon peninsula and on the northern coast of Hong Kong Island across the narrow strait of Kowloon Bay. Squeezing a new high rise into such tightly compressed areas is an enormous challenge for builders. The world-famous American architect I.M. Pei, commissioned to design a new skyscraper block in Hong Kong, said later it took him the better part of a year just to figure out how to get cars through a maze of narrow alleys and to the site.

The climate in Hong Kong is semitropical, resembling somewhat the climate found in Florida. But unlike Florida, Hong Kong's weather is controlled by the monsoons, seasonal winds that affect the climate in much of Asia. Cool, dry winds flow out of the northeast from October to April. From May through September the winds blow from the southwest, bringing the rainy season.

Working men and women can relax in Charter Park on Hong Kong Island.

October through December is the best time to visit Hong Kong. Days are warm, nights cool, and humidity low. Things change dramatically in January and February, with temperatures dipping into the mid-40s. While these winter days rarely reach the freezing point, the evenings often require that a person bundle up for warmth.

A mosaic design adds distinction to an office building in Kowloon.

High-rise apartment buildings house the large middle-class population of Hong Kong.

From May through September there are regular drenchings, and at the height of the summer, days and nights are marked by intense, muggy heat. This is also typhoon season. Hurricane-like storms can hit Hong Kong with winds topping 100 miles per hour, sending torrents of water racing down steep, narrow streets. Fortunately, these disturbances rarely strike the city head-on, but they come close enough to shut down airports, streets, and businesses. Even in ordinary years, Hong Kong's summer rainfall is about 85 inches, more than twice what New York gets in a year.

THE PAST

"Hong Kong investors should put their hearts at ease."

—Deng Xiaoping,
Chairman of the Communist Party,
the People's Republic of China

A traditional Chinese fan dance performed by young Hong Kong women.

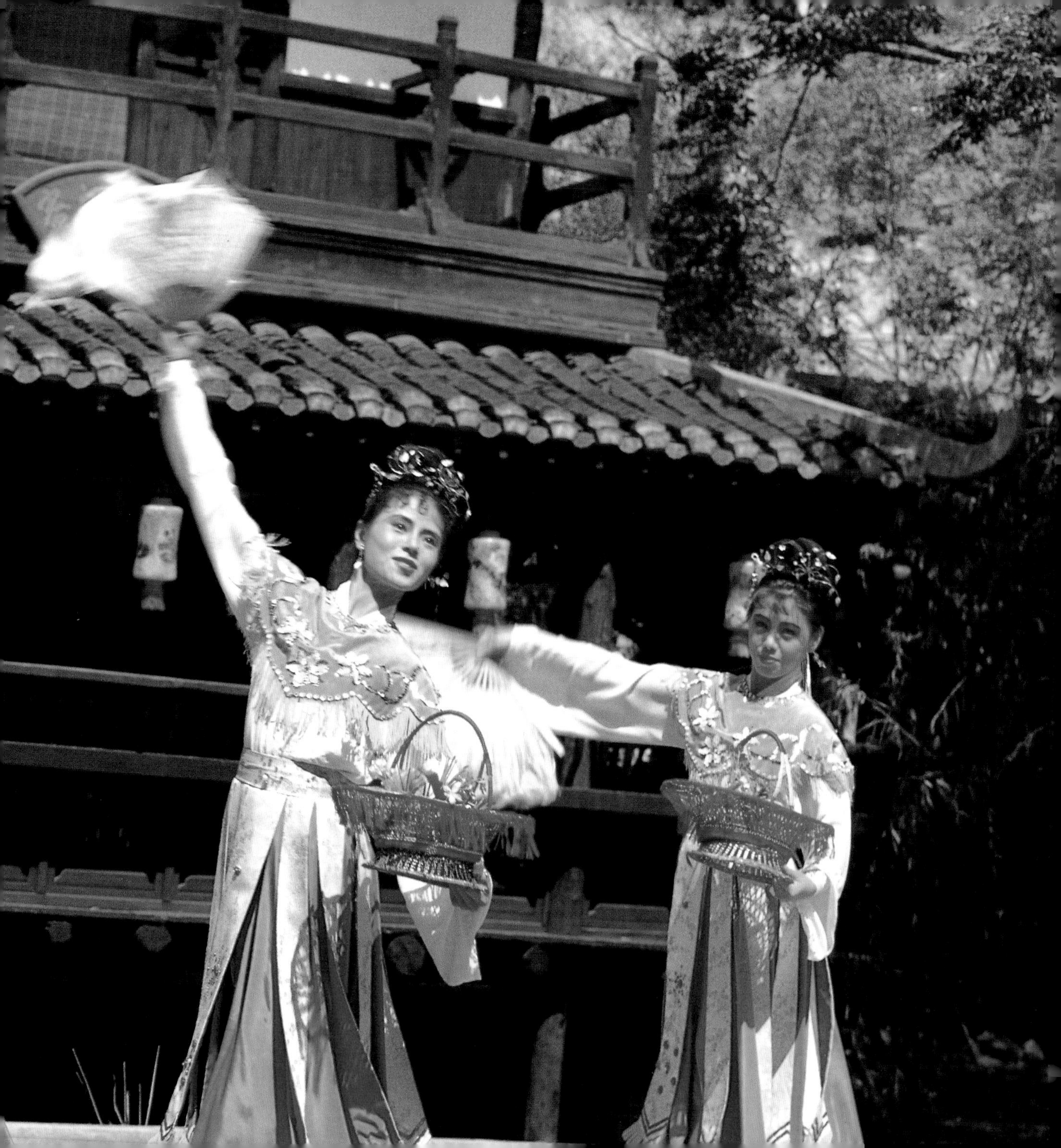

Hong Kong's status as a great city seems improbable, given its history. Consider these points: it was founded largely on sea piracy; almost half its people have no ancestral connection with Hong Kong; it has no natural resources, yet it is the wealthiest city in Asia; it is an extravagant example of no-holds-barred capitalism, yet it exists within the territory of a communist nation; after domination for nearly a century and a half by people of another race and vastly different culture, Hong Kong is still as truly Chinese as its motherland, and some would argue more so.

Being different as a community is, in fact, an essential element of the Hong Kong story. Isolated by geography and political circumstances from the mainstream of its own country's history, the people of this area are long accustomed to going it alone. In effect, they have had to invent themselves—and do it over and over again as different masters have taken control of their destiny. When 1997 comes and the People's Republic of China takes possession and control of the territory, Hong Kongers will be challenged yet again to demonstrate their skill as survivors.

Little is known about the early occupants of the Hong Kong region. The very earliest people (c. 6000 B.C.) were not Chinese at all, but rather aboriginals of a group called the Yao. Whether due to some natural disaster or to conquest, we do not know, but the Yao vanished thousands of years ago. They were replaced by the ancient race now known as the Chinese. In time, the widely scattered Chinese people and their countless warlords all came under the domain of the first emperors of Imperial China, who ruled their vast empire from behind the walls of the Forbidden City in Beijing. Since the people of Hong Kong lived 1,500 miles from Beijing and communication between them and the capital was difficult, the Imperial government had little effect on their lives, and the same was true of the outside world in general.

This situation began to change in the thirteenth century when Duan Zong, a child-emperor of the Sung Dynasty, fled from Beijing ahead of invading Mongols to seek safety in the mountains of Kowloon peninsula, north of Hong Kong. His flight was in vain; nine-year-old Duan Zong and his guards were hunted down and slain.

When the emperor intruded into the region during the seventeenth century, the effects were even more devastating. The Great Evacuation took place when the then-ruling Manchus, at war with the island people of Taiwan, moved the 16,000 people of the region inland and burned to the ground all coastal farms and houses so enemy troops coming ashore would find no food or shelter. The Taiwanese did not come, and the only sufferers from the emperor's "scorched earth" policy were his own people.

As the nineteenth century opened, the far-off emperor's presence was marked only by a few provincial officials, some troops and fortifications, and a couple of warships. The people of Hong Kong had achieved a stable way of life. They governed their own affairs in large measure, kept detailed legal records, enjoyed traveling theater companies, and entertained foreign visitors. A distinguished visitor from Beijing remarked with surprise on the relatively high level of learning and sophistication of the local population: "Culture has spread even to this remote place by the sea."

The main occupations in the region were rice farming, salt production, fishing, quarrying, incense gathering—and piracy. This last occupation was made easier by the coast's many bays and inlets and the hundreds of tiny nearby islands, where the marauders could hide between attacks. But the peninsula's magnificent deep-water harbor held the key to Hong Kong's future. It was, and still is, continually busy with the comings and goings of the ships of many nations.

Great Britain was at that time the dominant nation in the world and its ships the most active in commerce. To its shame, the majority of these vessels arrived from India with cargo-holds full of opium, or "foreign mud" as the local people called it, which was then turned over to Chinese middlemen for sale to the mainland population.

Engraving of a traditional ceremony honoring a graduate.

In time, opium use became so widespread and damaging to the Chinese people that it was hurting the country's economy. In 1839, a newly appointed Chinese official, on orders from Beijing, banned all opium imports and destroyed 20,291 chests of the drug that the British had in warehouses. In London, these actions were seized on as a good reason for British military action against imperial China.

A nineteenth-century painting depicting a sea battle between government gunboats and pirates.

British warships, bent on eliminating all harassment of British merchants and their trade in opium, soon attacked and subdued the local military. The Chinese were forced to negotiate for peace.

The commander of the victorious British fleet demanded that China transfer title to Hong Kong, a small, treeless island located one mile off the shore of the peninsula. Hong Kong was to be a permanent British military base, free port, and entry point for trade with China. On June 26, 1843, Hong Kong formally became a British Crown Colony, the first of a succession of bits of Chinese territory that foreigners would seize. A London newspaper cele-

By 1785, Hong Kong was already an established trading center.

brated the acquisition with these words: "Hong Kong—deep water and a free port for ever!"

After a later military conflict, the Convention of Peking ceded to the British tiny Stonecutters Island, near Hong Kong, and the southern part of Kowloon peninsula. In 1898, their holdings were expanded to include the remainder of Kowloon peninsula and hundreds of offshore islands, henceforth to be known collectively as the New Territories. These latter acquisitions were obtained not by absolute title but under a 99-year lease lasting until 1997. Since the island of Hong Kong could not be defended or sustained without possession of the New Territories, this agreement effectively set in place a terminal date for British rule over Hong Kong as well.

The British arrived in Hong Kong with high hopes for achieving profitable business results, but after a century of colonial possession, the British colony still had not realized its potential. Agriculture on land, trade by sea—these were the two cornerposts of Hong Kong's economy, but neither produced enough income to promote real growth in the region.

When the British subsequently abolished the opium trade, Hong Kong lapsed into the doldrums as a trade port. This condition continued until after the successful Chinese communist revolution of 1949. At that time, refugees from the mainland

English and Chinese advertisements light up Hong Kong's streets.

provided the community with an invaluable infusion of talent and capital. Then in 1950, China took sides with North Korea in the Korean War, declaring war against the United Nations. In response, the United Nations, including the United States, declared a total embargo on all trade with China and, because Hong Kong was so closely associated with China, against it as well. This had a devastating effect on the colony since the United States was one of Hong Kong's two largest trading partners, Great Britain being the other. Not only did the embargo block sales of the colony's products, it also cut Hong Kong off from needed supplies of raw materials and production machinery. By the end of the year, with unemployment high and refugees from the mainland flocking in, Hong Kong's economic situation looked desperate.

Amazingly, the solution to Hong Kong's problems came from the ranks of the refugees. This group included numbers of rich individuals who had brought substantial wealth with them when they fled the large mainland cities of Nanking, Canton, and Beijing, and now sought to invest that money. Other individuals possessed high levels of technical skill. Most importantly, the major body of refugees represented a vast pool of earnest, hard-working labor, ready to work for the free-world's lowest wages. To capitalist entrepreneurs, these were the perfect ingredients for new business ventures, which came into being at an astonishing rate. Within a decade, Hong Kong's economy grew to a point where the colony became one of Asia's largest manufacturing centers.

The "Made in Hong Kong" imprint now appears on a huge range of products in widely diverse categories. Microcomputers and other data processing products, industrial and consumer electronics, garments, air conditioners, electric appliances, and a long list of other goods sail out of Hong Kong harbor each day on ships bound for ports around the world. The companies that produce these products range in size. There are giant plants as modern as any in the world, down to hundreds of tiny factories located in Hong Kong's tenement districts, and operated in many cases by members of a single family.

In Hong Kong, the traditional and the modern often stand in sharp contrast to one another.

For five hundred years, junk boats like this one have transported freight and passengers in and around Hong Kong harbor.

In the last decade of the twentieth century, a cloud hangs over the colony as it faces the impending take-over by the communist People's Republic of China. In 1984, London signed an agreement with the communist government in Beijing, ceding to the Chinese full title to Hong Kong Island and the southern tip of Kowloon peninsula, also effective in 1997. The

Traditional Chinese temples are found amid the modern skyscrapers of Hong Kong.

mainland Chinese government agreed to allow Hong Kong—which will be known as Xianggang once it is under Chinese dominion—to operate as a capitalist and self-governing region until 2047. Meanwhile, the two governments agreed to draw up a constitution, to be known as The Basic Laws, under which the new state of Hong Kong will govern itself independently—for 50 years.

Repulse Bay Temple statue.

The brutal crackdown in June, 1989, on pro-democracy groups in China made Hong Kong citizens painfully aware that they could be subject to the same repression after 1997. Skilled professionals began leaving the colony at such a great rate that projections of Hong Kong's economic growth had to be cut in half. As the takeover date draws nearer, Hong Kong's businessmen and poor people alike have become increasingly uneasy about the colony's future prospects as a paradise of rags-to-riches free enterprise.

THE PEOPLE

"...a combination of British arrogance and Chinese apathy."

—Anonymous

Chinese opera performer applying his make-up.

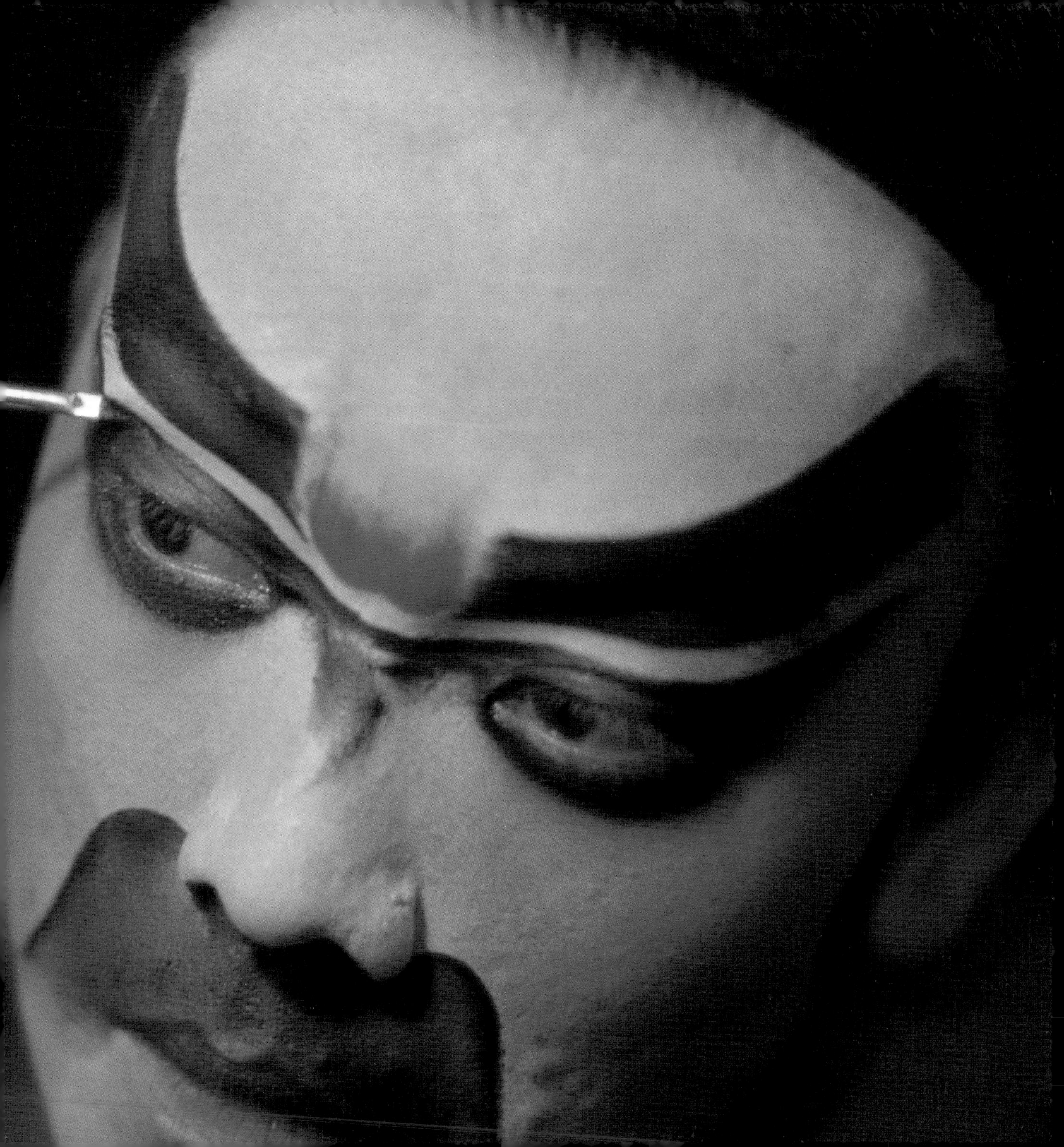

The early Chinese population (c. 5000 B.C.) of what we now call Hong Kong was made up of four mutually antagonistic tribal groups: the Punti, now known as the Cantonese; the Hoklos; the Hakkas, or "stranger families"; and an oppressed and outcast group called the Tankas, a name that translates as "egg people" and is possibly based on the egg-shaped canopies of Tankas boats. Because of their skill as farmers, the Cantonese families were the leading landowners and most powerful of the four Chinese groups, and they retain their dominance even today.

Members of these four ancient groups are still present in Hong Kong. One sees Hakkas women peering out from under traditional black-edged, wide straw hats, and Hoklos and Tankas families living near the sea as they have for thousands of years. And everywhere, there are the Cantonese and their language.

Almost half the people in Hong Kong came there from elsewhere. Most came from China's adjoining Guangdong Province, but a small number hail from almost every other part of the globe. This group, a fraction of Hong Kong's population, consists of British, French, German, Portuguese, and a scattering of other European nationalities, as well as Filipinos, Russians, Japanese, Indians, Australians, and a sprinkling of Americans. Filipinos constitute the largest non-Chinese population group.

Despite the influence of foreigners, 98 percent of the people in Hong Kong are Chinese. But there is a Chinese presence that involves much more than just numbers. A good example of this Chinese presence is to be found in the belief system *fung-shui,* which translates as "wind-water." It is an extremely ancient part of Chinese culture, probably older than any of their religions. It involves creating good luck. To create good luck you must find and respect a proper harmony and balance between yourself as a human being and the place where you find yourself. The practice of *fung-shui* is found everywhere: in the siting of a grave, to assure peace in the hereafter for the deceased, in the locating of a house, even in the positioning of a new skyscraper and the selection of specific angles at which its escalators and front doors are set.

Practitioners of *fung-shui,* known as geomancers, measure the complex information of this old belief and interpret it for their clients. The ranks of geomancers include people from the most uneducated workers to high-ranking corporate executives. It is interesting to note that *fung-shui's* concern for harmony between man and nature is also central to the beliefs and philosophy of Native Americans and many other cultures around the world.

However, the Chinese, Hong Kongers included, are historically not much interested in the cultural beliefs of others, shared or otherwise. They feel an

Tai chi, or shadow boxing, is practiced every morning in Hong Kong's parks as an aid to meditation and a way of achieving spiritual balance.

intense pride in China's heritage, aware that their ancestors were advanced in science and other areas of learning when Europeans and other peoples still lived in mud huts. The Chinese invented gunpowder when Europeans were developing the bow and arrow, and they used moveable type centuries before a German printer first made use of it in Europe. Eminent Chinese sages, most notably the philosopher Confucius, were read, discussed, and their teachings practiced centuries before those of many Western scholars.

Long ago, Chinese pride gradually became a closed-minded attitude in which all foreign peoples were looked on as being barbarians, incapable of teaching anything useful to China. This attitude was painfully tested during the nineteenth century by China's crushing defeats at the hands of various Western powers. Ever practical, the Chinese in modern times opened their minds to the usefulness of Western technology, and young Chinese students proved themselves to be stunningly capable of absorbing and applying Western knowledge. Still, in their customs and lifestyle and habits, the Chinese of Hong Kong remain very much Chinese.

The traditional Chinese attitude of viewing one's family as the central institution of life still flourishes in Hong Kong. However, the Chinese have a different view of the family than the one familiar to most Americans. Their families include parents, grand-

A modern performance of the traditional Chinese lion dance.

parents, uncles and aunts, cousins, nieces and nephews—whether close or distant. The head of this extended family is recognized to be its most senior male member, and his word is law regarding family decisions. This arrangement is consistent with the tradition that younger family members must respect their elders—a son obeys his father and older brothers, and a daughter, her mother and older sisters.

Another distinctive characteristic of the Chinese family is the fact that it presents a single, united front to the outside world, particularly in matters

Fan-making is a well-developed art in Hong Kong.

In Sung Dynasty Village, women are dressed in traditional clothing, holding pink fabric roses.

concerning the family's reputation and honor. Traditionally, offensive behavior by one family member casts lasting shame on the entire family, and over the centuries this viewpoint has served as a powerful check on irresponsible actions.

Until recent times, marriages of all young Chinese couples in Hong Kong were arranged by the elders in their respective families, without consulting the prospective bride and groom. A hired middleman would arbitrate all details, such as dowry, with the elders of both families. The young man and woman would not even meet for the first time until the very

Tiger Balm Gardens, Hong Kong.

day of their wedding, when the bride-to-be would arrive at her husband's house and pay homage to him and his venerable ancestors. Today, many modern Chinese couples in Hong Kong ignore the old ways, selecting and marrying a mate of their own choice in Western-style ceremonies.

As much or perhaps more than with any other culture, children are the "glue" that holds together the structure of the Chinese family. The Chinese love large families, and while the government on the mainland has permitted most couples to have only one child or at the most two, it is not uncommon for Hong Kong Chinese families to have five, six, or seven children. While the birth of a first son has traditionally been a matter of particular rejoicing, even this perception of relative human value has changed as Chinese women have achieved higher education and won meaningful positions in business and government.

In their general level of education, the majority of Hong Kong women lag behind men. At last report, little more than 58 percent of women were literate compared with a figure of over 90 percent of men. These figures reflect both the relative unconcern traditionally felt in Chinese families about educating daughters and the large numbers of illiterate refugees who have flooded into the colony.

The rickshaw is often an effective taxi in Hong Kong's crowded streets.

Still, education is recognized as being the surest road to success in Hong Kong's competitive economic system. Educational achievers are rewarded with better job opportunities and put on the fast track toward good promotions. So the Hong Kong government, mindful of the needs of business and industry, committed itself to an all-out program of school construction, both public and private. Unlike the United States, education is not available free in Hong Kong—all parents must pay tuition. Free tuition is available for some poor children whose parents cannot afford the tuition, but certainly not for all, and especially not for most children in refugee camps.

In most of the elementary schools, Cantonese is the language in which instruction is given, while English is taught as a second language. However, in most of the colony's high schools, all teaching is done in English, a clear reflection of the importance

Hong Kongers enthusiastically support the rugby competition.

to Hong Kong of its trade with the world's two largest English-speaking nations, Great Britain and the United States. Also, fluency in English is a requirement for admission to the colony's British-sponsored University of Hong Kong, where only English is spoken. Many international scholars feel the university is one of the best in Asia.

Traditionally, the hard-working Chinese have had little time to spare for game sports. When the British first arrived in Hong Kong in the last century and demonstrated their passionate interest in such field games as soccer, rugby, and cricket, the Chinese were at first less interested in the games than they were puzzled and amused by actions of "the crazy barbarians." But as Western ways caught on, this attitude changed. Today, there are many soccer teams in Hong Kong, some of them good enough to engage in international competition. And basketball has become a popular pastime in the colony; government-built courts in public parks are in constant use.

One cannot talk about recreation in Hong Kong without mentioning the table game of mah jongg. Played with 152 tiles marked with Chinese characters and resembling dominoes, it is a mentally challenging game. Walking through the narrow, winding streets of Hong Kong, a visitor will see men at sidewalk tables everywhere engaged in the game and hear from house windows the distinctive clicking of mah jongg tiles.

Undoubtedly because Hong Kongers have devoted themselves much more to the cultivation of fortunes than to the pursuit of humanistic graces, work and study in the fine arts has not been a strong point of the colony. While concerned individuals and organizations regularly present Western art, music, and theater, little work of note has been generated by Hong Kong's own artistic community. Critics attribute this lack of significant artistic output to the lack of a creative climate in the colony.

The art form most popular among Hong Kong residents is an ancient one: Chinese theater, also known as Chinese opera. In addition to presentations in indoor theaters, one can see Chinese opera groups performing outdoors during many festivals. Musicians, often casually clad in T-shirts and jeans, play instruments such as cymbals and drums, while performers in elaborate costumes and with heavily made-up faces act out the ancient plots of love and derring-do. And all the while the audience acts, to Western eyes, more as though they were attending a wrestling match than an opera. They shout warnings and advice to heroes and boo the villains. (In American cowboy movies, the villain traditionally wears a black hat; in Chinese opera, he's the one with a red spot on his forehead.)

Hong Kong is one of the world's leading production centers for motion pictures. Its films—more than 300 a year—are shown mainly in Asian countries

Tourists enjoy a scenic overlook of Hong Kong's famous harbor.

with large Chinese populations, mainland China excepted. The plots of the films invariably promote traditional values—often expressed through martial-arts violence—making them a particularly good example of how the Chinese will adopt Western ways when it can be used to serve their own cultural heritage.

Green jade is the material most favored by Chinese craftsmen.

The best known of all the traditional Chinese art forms is their handicrafts, and much of this work is done in Hong Kong. In addition to jade carvings, Hong Kong artists produce intricate ivory carvings made from elephant tusks. Very likely we will be seeing the last of these carvings on the legal market, for the international community, aroused by the threat to the endangered African elephant, has prohibited the sale of elephant ivory and ivory products.

While a half million Hong Kongers are Christians or Muslims, by far the largest percentage of citizens are Taoists, Confucianists, or Buddhists. It is important to understand that Taoism and Confucianism are not so much religions, as Westerners understand religions to be, as they are philosophies of harmonious behavior.

Taoism originated with Lao-tze, who is believed to have lived in the seventh century B.C. A book

Bronze incense burner from the Sung Dynasty which lasted from A.D. 960-1280.

ascribed to Lao-tze, the *Tao-te-ching* or "Book of the Way and of Virtue," teaches that feelings and instincts, not intellectual analysis, are one's proper guides to living the virtuous life and thus achieving salvation. The simplicity and modesty of *the way,* as it was called, appealed enormously to the Chinese people, and over the centuries Taoism spread widely. Today, Taoism is not one unified belief but many, incorporating many popular superstitions, such as witchcraft, astrology, alchemy, and animism, in its rituals.

Confucius, born in 551 B.C. and a younger contemporary of Lao-tze, was himself a teacher and scholar. He urged honesty and fairness on nobles and high officials as the ideal way to improve human society, and he believed that people needed only to be properly educated to be fundamentally good. His philosophy, since known as Confucianism, was directed primarily to intellectuals, and it never caught on as a religion with the masses of Chinese, but Confucius himself is venerated by all and his wise teachings frequently quoted.

Unlike Taoism and Confucianism, Buddhism is not Chinese in origin but came instead from neighboring India. Buddhism differs too in that it includes a priesthood of monks, and it is through the prayers and intercessions of these monks, rather than by the actions of individual believers, that salvation is achieved.

Hong Kong schoolchildren study both Cantonese and English.

The more affluent people of Hong Kong buy their clothes in modern shopping malls.

The Chinese are very practical-minded, so it is quite understandable that they would have blended together bits and pieces of ritual observances from a number of religions—" just in case," as a Hong Konger might put it. This down-to-earth attitude toward religion reflects a clear-eyed Chinese way of seeing life not as one might *like* it to be but as, in fact, it truly is.

But while most Hong Kongers have a casual connection to religion, they enthusiastically observe a great number of religious ceremonies and festivals. For example, Hong Kong Chinese worship their ancestors, make burnt offerings when someone dies,

and have a geomancer select the grave site. In daily
life and business, they perform assorted rituals
aimed at soliciting the favors of "good" gods and
fending off the wrath of "bad" gods.

While Hong Kong possesses shopping malls and
supermarkets as modern as any in the West, the
majority of food shopping still is done at traditional
markets. These are found everywhere from one end

Causeway Bay runs into the heart of
Hong Kong's trading center.

of the crowded colony to the other. Wherever there are blocks of apartment towers or tenements, clusters of canopy-covered stalls and farmers' wagons gather to offer food for sale. Here one finds fruits and vegetables, some from the few remaining local farms; pigs and ducks from mainland China; and creatures taken from the nearby bay—crabs, eels, prawns, oysters. The entire village of Lau Fau Shan, on the peninsula's west coast, looks like one

Food plays a very important part in Chinese culture. It must not only taste good but be pleasing to the eye.

Western consumer goods are readily available in Hong Kong. They are often less expensive in Hong Kong because of its duty-free status.

mammoth seafood market, and people come from all over the colony to shop there.

Curiously, there have been few individuals in the history of Hong Kong who could properly have had the term "famous" assigned to them. The names of British governors are seen everywhere in the colony—on streets, squares, parks, avenues and districts. But Hong Kong stands out more for the extraordinariness of its whole population rather than for the fame of individuals. Not surprisingly, the great names in Hong Kong are those businessmen who have amassed great wealth, often as bankers, merchants, and shipping magnates. It is this dream of fabulous riches that is the engine that runs Hong Kong; and it is the Chinese native entrepreneurial spirit and adaptability that provides the fuel.

ON THE TOUR BUS

Museums

Art Gallery, Institute of Chinese Studies, Chinese University, Shatin, New Territories. Of special interest to Hong Kong's largely Cantonese Chinese population, the gallery displays a 300-year-long representation of works by artists from nearby Canton Province, together with such earlier artifacts as jade flower carvings, rubbings of pre-Christian inscriptions in stone, and imperial bronze seals.

Fung Ping Shan Museum, University of Hong Kong, 94 Bonham Road, Mid-Levels. A "must" for serious scholars of Chinese history, the museum houses the world's largest and most important collection of Nestorian Christian artifacts dating from the Yuan Dynasty period (1279-1644), and also such early pieces as ceremonial bowls, decorated pottery, and ornamental mirrors.

Hong Kong Museum of History, Haiphong Road, Kowloon Park, Tsimshatsui,

The Hong Kong Museum of History.

Kowloon—the museum to visit in Hong Kong. It offers a number of permanent collections representing local traditions and history, archaeology, and arts and crafts, along with well-presented temporary shows. There is also a magnificent photographic collection.

Hong Kong Museum of Art, 10th and 11th floors, City Hall High Block. An excellent collection of Chinese antiquities, especially paintings, drawings, and ceramics, along with a fascinating exhibit on the topic of Chinese-British relations in Hong Kong. Worth-

54

while special shows change each month.

Jade Museum, Aw Boon Haw Gardens, Tin Hang Road, Causeway Bay, Hong Kong. As its name suggests, this is a museum of jade pieces—in fact, it offers the finest jade collection in the world.

Lei Cheung Uk Museum, Tonkin Street, Lei Cheng Uk Resettlement Estate, Shamshuipo. First unearthed in 1955, this ancient burial vault, occupant unknown, dates from the Late Han Dynasty (A.D. 25-220). It consists of four brick-walled and barrel-shaped chambers laid out to form a cross around a central chamber. On display are typical funerary objects.

Museum of Chinese Historical Relics, Causeway Centre, 28 Harbour Road, Wanchai, Hong Kong. A modest but worthwhile

Kowloon, on the mainland, offers a fast-paced night life.

Hong Kong's Jumbo Floating Restaurant.

collection of ancient Chinese art objects and artifacts are exhibited here.

Museum of Tea Ware, Flagstaff House, Victoria Barracks, Queensway, Hong Kong. Operated by the Hong Kong Museum of Art, this new institution is the world's most comprehensive museum relating to the beverage, tea. Displays include a collection of Yi Xing teaware from the Ming Dynasty period and rare and beautiful tea sets from Jiangsu Province,

The Hong Kong Tea Museum.

Ferry), Hong Kong. Actually three libraries in one: the general reading library covers a universal range of topics; the children's library includes both Chinese and English volumes; and a remarkably complete reference library offers over 400,000 volumes, some in Chinese and some in English, as well as a good microfiche collection of Hong Kong newspapers and rare books in the Beijing Museum. Foreigners must show a passport to enter.

American Library, United Center, Queens Road, Central, Hong Kong. Readers can find new and back-dated American newspapers and magazines and

China. Also offered are slide shows and exhibits on the early tea trade, tea planting, brewing, and serving.

Hong Kong Space Museum, Salisbury Street, Tsimshatsui, Kowloon. A remarkably good collection of aerospace materials, highlighted by the Aurora 7 space capsule in which Scott Carpenter circled the planet three times back in 1962. Sophisticated audiovisual equipment and computers provide hands-on access to aerospace information. Of special interest is the Hall of Solar Sciences, complete with telescope.

Sung Dynasty Wax Museum, Sung Dynasty Village, 11 Kau Wa Heng, Laichikok, Kowloon. The basic collection of costumed wax mannequins covers life in the "golden age" of ancient Chinese culture, the Sung Dynasty (A.D. 960-1279); other collections represent 5000 years of Chinese culture.

Libraries

City Hall Libraries, City Hall High Block (close by Star

Hong Kong Stock Exchange.

phone directories for major U.S. cities.

Schools

Chinese University. An excellent institution that graduates many of Hong Kong's top executives and technicians. The university is near the dock from which a morning ferry sails to Tap Mun, a major island, and to fishing villages on the mainland.

Hong Kong University, Pokfulam Road, Hong Kong. The century-old buildings are a beehive of activity by very serious students. The university includes a museum and excellent library.

Hong Kong Academy for the Performing Arts, Harbor Road, Winchai, Hong Kong. A wonderful facility that includes two major theaters with a total seating of 1,600, an estimated 200-seat studio theater, and additional smaller studios.

Cultural Events & Festivals

Asian Arts Festival. A biennial celebration, two to three weeks in length, featuring performances by many prominent Asian artists. The festival is held in October and November biennially.

Chinese New Year Festival. A three-day festival ends with the *Yuen Siu (Lantern) Festival.* Beautiful lanterns are displayed

Salute to the Chinese New Year.

in homes and business places. The event's dates vary according to lunar phases from January to March.

Cheung Chau Bun Festival. The week-long Buddhist/Taoist celebration in May includes competition for specially baked lucky buns and the performing of Chinese street operas. The festival's traditional purpose is to pacify the ghosts of people once murdered by pirates.

Ching Ming Festival. In April, huge crowds gather at cemeteries as Chinese families visit and decorate ancestral graves.

Cheung Yueng Festival. A low-key, pleasant celebration of good luck, this October event is marked by families visiting ancestral gravesites and by picnics in parks and on beaches.

Dragon Boat Festival. Many dazzling races between colorful dragon boats, which are rowed to the loud beating of drums, take place in June.

Hong Kong Arts Festival. A month of dramatic and concert

During the Bun Festival, crowds gather to watch Chinese street opera.

The Dragon Boat Races attract competitors and spectators from all over the world.

performances held throughout Hong Kong in February-March.

Hungry Ghost Festival. A major event in August, it marks the occasion when the Yen Lo, or "hungry ghosts," are said to roam the earth. Celebrants burn special paper money and put food offerings at roadsides to placate the ethereal visitors.

International Film Festival. Two weeks of Asian, European, and American films in April.

Lord Buddha's Birthday. Colorful ceremonies are held in May at Buddhist temples; visitors are welcome.

Mid-Autumn Festival. Parks and beaches fill on festival night with people bearing food and colorful lanterns, all to celebrate the moon goddess. Held in September, it is the Hong Kong equivalent of harvest moon festivals.

Tin Hau Temple and Festival. Colorfully decorated fishing boats and on-shore dragon dances celebrate the Goddess of the Sea during May.

C H R O N O L O G Y

c. 6000 B.C.	Neolithic settlement of China during which the Yao people live in the territory of present-day Hong Kong.		Hong Kong under the Treaty of Nanking.
		1856	Kowloon and Stonecutters Island acquired by British.
c. 5000 B.C.	The Yao vanish, replaced by Chinese peoples.	1898	British lease New Territories from China for 99 years.
A.D. 1279	Duan Zong, a child emperor, flees Beijing to hide from invading Mongols; caught and slain.	1921	Kowloon-Guangzhou railroad completed; University of Hong Kong opens.
c. 1600	The Great Evacuation.		
1699	British East India Company establishes the first British trade relationship with China.	1941	Japanese invade and occupy Hong Kong.
		1945	Japan defeated, Hong Kong liberated.
1773	First British ships arrive in Chinese ports to trade.	1951	UN embargo placed on all Hong Kong goods.
1839	Chinese outlaw opium use, destroy British supplies.	1984	British agree to cede Hong Kong to China in 1997.
1842	British acquire title to		

FOR FURTHER READING

Burkhard, V.P. *Chinese Creeds and Customs.* S.C.M. Post, 1953.
Endacott, G.B. *A History of Hong Kong.* Oxford University Press, 1978.
Fodor's Hong Kong and Macau. Fodor's Travel Publications, 1988.
Hong Kong. Insight Guides. APA Productions, Ltd., 1986.
Le Carre, John. *The Honourable Schoolboy.* Alfred A. Knopf, 1970.
Morris, Jan. *Hong Kong.* Random House, 1988.
Warner, John. *Fragrant Harbour.* John Warner Publications, 1976.

WHERE TO GET MORE INFORMATION

Hong Kong Tourist Association Offices:
590 Fifth Avenue, 5th Floor
New York, NY 10036-4706
Tel: (212) 869-5008/9

Suite 2400, 333 N. Michigan Avenue
Chicago, IL 60601-3966
Tel: (312) 782-3872

10940 Wilshire Boulevard
Suite 1220
Los Angeles, CA 90024
Tel: (213) 208-4582

Suite 404, 360 Post Street
San Francisco, CA 94108
Tel: (415) 781-4775

Head Office:
35th Floor, Jardine House
1 Connaught Place, Central
Hong Kong
Tel: 5-244191

INDEX

Photo Credits

Cover, page 55: Jean-Paul Nacivet/Leo de Wys, Inc.; 3 (top, bottom), 7, 8-9, 29, 32-33, 35, 42, 46, 50, 52, 53, 54, 56 (left), 57, 58, 59: courtesy Hong Kong Tourist Authority; 3 (middle), 11, 16, 18-19: Van Phillips/Leo de Wys, Inc.; 4-5, 15, 17, 30, 31, 38, 39, 40, 45, 49, 55 (left): Steve Vidler/Leo de Wys, Inc.; 12-13: Reproduced by Kind Permission of the Hong Kong Government; 14, 41: Fridmar Damm/Leo de Wys, Inc.; 22: Special Collections Office, New York Public Library, Astor, Lenox, and Tilden Foundations; 23, 24: Reproduced by Permission of the Urban Council of Hong Kong, from the Collection of the Hong Kong Museum of Art; 26: John Lamb/Leo de Wys, Inc.; 28: Bob Thomason/Leo de Wys, Inc.; 37: Ashvin Gatha/Leo de Wys, Inc.; 47: Worcester Art Museum, Worcester, Massachusetts; 51: Casimir/Leo de Wys, Inc.; 56 (right): courtesy Hong Kong Economic and Trade Office.